Published by Creative Education
P.O. Box 227, Mankato, Minnesota 56002
Creative Education is an imprint of The Creative Company
www.thecreativecompany.us

Design by Blue Design
Production by The Design Lab
Printed in the United States of America

Photographs by Alamy (Ace Stock Limited, Imagebroker, ImageState, Visual & Written SL, John Warburton-Lee Photography), iStockphoto (Adam Borkowski, Wojciech Gajda, Bill Grove, Steve Lovegrove, Andrew Manley, Chris Seredon, Freddie Vargas, Josh Webb, Dusan Zidar)

Copyright © 2009 Creative Education
International copyright reserved in all countries. No part of this book may be reproduced in any form without written permission from the publisher.

Library of Congress Cataloging-in-Publication Data

Bodden, Valerie.
Running / by Valerie Bodden.
p. cm. — (Active sports)
Includes index.
ISBN 978-1-58341-700-3
1. Running—Juvenile literature. I. Title.

GV1061.B63 2009
613.7'172—dc22   2007051577

First Edition
9 8 7 6 5 4 3 2 1

Running

Valerie Bodden

The breeze blows across your face. You breathe in and out, in and out. You move your legs faster and faster. Running makes you feel great!

Runners have to take deep breaths as they run.

People have run in races for thousands of years.

People around the world like to run. Some people run to get places. Other people run for exercise or for fun. And some people run in races. The best runners in the world race in the **Olympics**.

Many races are held on **tracks**. Some track races are short. Racers run as fast as they can. Short, fast races are called sprints. One of the fastest sprinters in the world is Asafa (*uh-SAH-fuh*) Powell. One time, he ran 100 meters (110 yards) in 9.74 seconds!

Sprinters like Asafa Powell pump their arms back and forth.

Other track races are long. Racers do not run at top speed for most of the race. They save their energy to finish the race. When they get close to the finish line, they run as fast as they can.

Some runners jump over gates called hurdles as they run.

RUNNING

About 20,000 people run in the Boston Marathon every year.

Some races are not on tracks. They are on roads. Long races called marathons are usually run on roads. Marathons are 26.2 miles (42.2 km) long. They take most people about three hours to run! One of the most famous marathons is called the Boston Marathon.

Some races are even longer than marathons. They are called ultra marathons. The longest ultra marathon is 3,100 miles (4,990 km) long!

Cross-country runners run through woods, fields, and hills.

RUNNING

In a relay race, runners are part of a team.

Runners do not need a lot of **equipment** (*ee-KWIP-ment*). The main thing they need is a good pair of running shoes. The shoes have to fit well. If they do not, they will hurt the runner's feet.

Runners need comfortable clothes, too. Runners wear cool clothes in the summer. They wear warmer clothes in the winter.

Drivers have to be careful of people running on the road.

20

RUNNING

Before they start to run, runners walk around and stretch. After they are done running, runners walk and stretch again. This helps keep their **muscles** (*MUSS-uhls*) from getting sore. That way, they will be ready to run again soon!

Runners have to drink plenty of water to stay healthy.

RUNNING

GLOSSARY

equipment—tools or gear to make something easier or safer

muscles—parts of the body that help people move

Olympics—a sports contest for people from around the world; there are lots of different sports included

tracks—oval-shaped paths made for running

INDEX

clothes 18, 19
exercise 7
hurdles 10
marathons 12, 13, 14
Olympics 7
Powell, Asafa 8, 9
races 7, 16, 22
running shoes 17
sprints 8
stretching 21
tracks 8
ultra marathons 14